D1085636

GRAND ROYAL PALACES OF KOREA

Over 200 Pages of Beautiful Photos With Cultural and Historical Background Explanations In English

by Yeong-hun Lee and Brian Wilson

ISBN : 9791188195541

reach us at : marketing@newampersand.com

Printed in the United States of America

Table of Contents

continued on the next page

경복궁 Gyeongbokgung

Meaning "palace greatly blessed by heaven", Gyeongbokgung was built three years after the Joseon Dynasty 조선왕조 (1392-1897) was founded and it served as its main palace ever since then.

With Mount Bugak 북악산 as a backdrop and the Street of Six Ministries (today's Sejong-no 세종로) outside Gwanghwamun Gate 광화문, the main entrance to the palace, Gyeongbokgung was situated in the heart of the Korean capital city. It was steadily expanded before being reduced to ashes during the Japanese invasion of 1592.

For the next 273 years, the palace grounds were left derelict until being rebuilt in 1867 under the leadership of Regent Heungseon Daewongun 흥선대원군. The restoration was completed on a grand scale, with 330 buildings crowded together in a labyrinthine configuration.

Within the palace walls were *oejeon* 외전 ("outer court"), offices for the king and state officials, and *naejeon* 내전 ("inner court"), which included living quarters for the royal family as well as gardens for leisure. Within its extensive precincts were other palaces, large and small, including Junggung 중궁 (the Queen's residence) and Donggung 동궁(the Crown Prince's residence).

Due to its status as the symbol of national sovereignty, Gyeongbokgung was demolished during the Japanese occupation of the early 20th century. In 1911, ownership of land at the palace was transferred to the Japanese Governor-General. In 1915, on the pretext of holding an exhibition, more than 90% of the buildings were torn down. Following the exhibition, the Japanese leveled whatever still remained and built their colonial headquarters, the Government-General Building (1916–26), on the site.

Restoration efforts have been ongoing since 1990. The Government-General Building was removed in 1996 and Heungnyemun Gate 흥례문(2001) and Gwanghwamun Gate (2006-2010) were reconstructed in their original locations and forms. Reconstructions of the Inner Court and Crown Prince's residence have also been completed.

광화문 Gwanghwamun

Gwanghwamun, meaning "spreading light" is the main and largest gate of Gyeongbokgung. First constructed in 1395 as the main gate to Gyeongbokgung, it served as a landmark and symbol of Seoul's long history as the capital city during the Joseon Dynasty. The gate has gone through multiple periods of destruction and disrepair. During the 1592 Japanese invasion, it was destroyed by fire and left in ruins for over 250 years. Restoration work on the gate was finished and it was opened to the public on August 15, 2010.

It was reconstructed in 1867 along with the rest of Gyeongbokgung Palace. The gate stood until 1926, when the Japanese government had it deconstructed and moved it just to the southeast of the current location of the National Folk Museum of Korea to make way for the massive Japanese Governor General Building

The Korean War completely destroyed the wooden structure of Gwanghwamun, and its stone base lay in complete disrepair and neglect. In 1968, during 박정희 Park Chung-hee's administration, the stone base was again relocated in front of the Japanese Governor General Building. The destroyed wooden structure was rebuilt in concrete, while the sign on Gwanghwamun was written in hangul by Park himself. Gwanghwamun remained as a concrete gate until late 2006.

Haetae 해태, or *haechi* 해치 is a legendary creature in Chinese and Korean mythology. According to Korean records, *Haetae*'s body is muscular, and shaped like a lion and has a horn on its forehead. It has a bell in its neck, and the body is covered with sharp scales. It lives in the frontier areas of Manchuria. In ancient Korea, *Haetae* sculptures were used in architecture during the early Joseon dynasty, as their image was trusted to be able to protect Hanyang 한양 (now Seoul) from natural disasters and to give law and order among the populace.

11

동십자각 Dongsipjagak

Dongsipjagak was originally connected with the wall of Gyeongbokgung, as it served as a watchtower on which the guards climbed to stand on guard, using stairs. The roof, called *yeojang* 여장, shut out the rain and provided protection from enemies' arrows and bullets, making it an excellent combat facility. But during the Japanese occupation, the east wall of Gyeongbokgung was severely damaged, and also to broaden the front road, this watchtower had to be removed from the body of Gyeongbokgung, and has been standing apart from the rest, like a lonely island. On the roof, there are japsang statues and dancheong decorations, which are only allowed on palace roofing, suggesting that this is a palace building.

기별청 Gibyeolcheong

Gibyeolcheong served as a modern day post office inside the palace, standing adjacent to Yuhwamun, a gate where the government officials had to wait before the arranged time to meet the king. Thanks to its location, this little building played the role of delivering *gibyeolji* 기별지, something that can be likened to a newsletter, which contained important tasks for the day, to the government officials so they are informed of the current issues the king may be interested in knowing.

신무문 Sinmumun (The North Gate, above)

Meaning "gate of outstanding military prowess and courage", Sinmumun is the north gate of Gyeongbokgung. According to traditional yin-yang ideology, the north symbolizes winter and death and is strongly yin. For this reason, the north gate always remained locked to keep the yin of the north gate from disturbing the inside of the palace. There were, however, rare occasions on which this gate was opened. It was opened during shaman services held to pray for rain during a drought and when the king wanted to go to the archery field at what is today known as Cheongwadae, the residence of the president of South Korea. By the decree of the South Korean presidential office, the gate stayed locked for security purposes until it was opened in 2006 for public viewing.

건춘문 Geonchunmun (The East Gate, right, above)

Meaning "the gate where Spring begins", Geonchunmun is the east gate of Gyeongbokgung, and those who could pass through the gate were the crown prince, the royal family, and the royal family in-laws. In February 1896, the last king of Joseon, King Gojong 고종, escaped the palace through this gate, five months after his wife Queen Myeongseong 명성황후 had been assassinated by a Japanese assassin. He escaped to the Russian legation on a palanquin being used by court ladies. King Gojong never returned to Gyeongbokgung.

영춘문 Yeongchunmun (The West Gate, below)

Meaning "the gate that welcomes the Autumn", Yeongchumun is the west gate of Gyeongbokgung, and was used by the officials who worked in government offices inside the palace. Early in the Joseon period, a prince's uprising occurred inside Gyeongbokgung, as he was resentful of his half-brother being designated as the crown prince. He devised a plan with his corroborators and held many secret meetings. The members are said to have entered the palace through this gate. Yeonsangun 연산군, known as the most atrocious tyrant in Joseon history, loved to hold lavish banquets at Gyeonghoeru 경회루, and to prevent people from coming in, he ordered to have the gate blocked up using thorns. He would then entertain himself by sailing on boats in the pond.

흥례문 Heungnyemun (The Second Inner Gate)

Meaning "gate of promoting proprieties", Heungnyemun, is the second gate into Gyeongbokgung. Gatekeepers stood on duty for two-hour shifts at the gate, whose reenactment takes place at the same location today, according to the rules laid out by the book titled ugiwe, which records the order and format of state ceremonies in Joseon, and this is also part of UNESCO's Memory of the World programme.

The gate was torn down during the Japanese occupation, and Government-General building was built there, in an attempt to block Korean people from seeing the palace, the symbol of their country. In 1995, the Korean government tore down the building, which had been used as a museum after libration in 1945, and rebuilt and restored the gate.

흥례문 Heungnyemun (The Second Inner Gate)

근정문 Geunjeongmun (Third Inner Gate)

Geunjeongmun Gate 근정문 opens up into Throne Hall, Geunjeongjeon. In the middle of the steps you can find a stone carved into the shape of the phoenix, which is a legendary creature that was said to only appear during a peaceful and prosperous reign, and also symbolizes the king. The location on which the phoenix is carved is also along down the king's path. According to tradition, the king does not walk on the ground. Thus, the king's palanquin would pass over this spot.

삼도 Samdo

Upon passing through Heungnyemun, you are faced with a path divided into three sections, known as *samdo* ("three paths"). The central path, widest and highest among them, is the royal path, called *eodo* 어도, which was used exclusively by the kings. The east path was used by civil officials and the west path by military officials.

행각 Haenggak (Corridor)

The **행각** *haenggak* of Geunjeongjeon surrounds the building to the east, west, south, and north. It forms a perfect symmetry around the building and **근정문** Geunjeongmun.

융문루 Yungmunnu and **융무루** Yungmuru are projected to the outside at the 17th and 18th **칸** kans from the south on the **동행각** Donghaenggak ("east corridor") and **서행각** Seohaenggak ("west corridor").

Furthermore, at the left and right of **남행각** Namhaenggak ("south corridor") and Geunjeongmun are **일화문** Ilhwamun and **월화문** Wolhwamun, respectively, to allow people to enter and exit without passing through the Geunjeongmun.

근정전 Geunjeongjeon

Originally constructed in 1395 during the reign of King Taejo 태
조, it's the throne hall where the king formally granted audiences to
his officials, gave declarations of national importance, and greeted
foreign envoys and ambassadors during the Joseon Dynasty. It was
burned down in 1592 during the Japanese invasion, the building was
restored in 1867. The name, given by the minister Jeong Do-jeon 정도
전, means "diligence helps governance". Constructed mainly of wood,
Geunjeongjeon sits on the center of a large rectangular courtyard, on top
of a two-tiered stone platform.

This two-tiered platform is lined with detailed balustrades and is
decorated with numerous sculptures depicting imaginary and real
animals, such as dragons and phoenixes. The stone-paved courtyard
is lined with two rows of rank stones, called pumgyeseoks, indicating
where the court officials are to stand according to their ranks.
The whole courtyard is fully enclosed by wooden cloisters.

어좌 Eojwa

The Phoenix Throne (*eojwa* 어좌) is the English term used to identify the throne of the hereditary monarchs of Korea. In an abstract sense, the Phoenix Throne also refers rhetorically to the head of state of the Joseon dynasty (1392–1897) and the Empire of Korea (*daehan jeguk*) 대한제국 (1897–1910).

The Phoenix motif symbolizes the king's supreme authority. The phoenix has a long association with Korean royalty — for example, in Goguryeo 고구려 tomb murals like that of the Middle Gangseo Tumulus where the painted image of a phoenix is featured.

Enthronement ceremonies and the throne itself has evolved across the span of Korean history. For example, from 1399–1549, seven of twelve kings were enthroned in the royal throne hall (Geunjeong-jeon) at Gyeongbokgung Palace. In other words, Jeongjong 정종, Sejong 세종, Danjong 단종, Sejo 세조, Seongjong 성종, Jungjong 중종, and Myeongjong 명종 ascended the Phoenix Throne in the same royal location.

The portrait of Gojong, king of Josen Dynasty.
Lithography by Joseph de la Nezière from l'Extrême Orient en Image published in 1903.

일월오봉도 Irworobongdo

Irworobongdo is a Korean folding screen with a highly stylized landscape painting of the sun and moon, five peaks which always was set behind *eojwa*, the king's royal throne during the Joseon Dynasty. It literally means "Painting of the Sun, Moon and the Five Peaks" and is also called "*Irwoldo* 일월도" or "*Irwolgonryundo* 일월곤륜도". The sun and moon symbolize the king and queen while the five peaks denote a mythical place. The screen serves to display the majesty of the Joseon royal court.

The scene depicts a burning red sun, a full moon, five craggy peaks, and two fast-flowing streams with cascades, all flanked by a pair of conifers. The brilliant colours — known as *tang-chae* 탕채 (Chinese colours) — were fixed with either animal or fish glue, rendering the screens brilliant and waterfast. New York Times critic Holland Cotter has described the screen's solid, saturated colors and robust forms as being regular as "textile patterns", and noted that these screens have "an archaic, hieratic look unlike Chinese or Japanese painting of the time."

There are no existing documents from an early period to explain the original iconography of the Five Peaks. Chadwick reports the findings of Dr. Yi Song-mi, Professor of Art History at the Academy of Korean Studies in Seoul. He has suggested that these screens were one of the most important elements in the throne hall, and that this formalized landscape illustrates the Joseon political cosmology. The "almost" red sun represents the king as the yang, the positive male principle, while the white moon represents the queen as the yin, the negative female principle. These two principles make the universe work.

An alternative explanation is that the screen might represent the blessing of Korea by Heaven, symbolized by the sun and moon in balance. When the king sat in front of this screen, he appeared to be at the pivotal point from which all force emanated and to which all returned. Thus, imbued with sacred power, the screen manifests a political cosmology as evidence of Heaven's favor, mandate, and continued protection of the ruler.

사정전 Sajeongjeon

Sajeongjeon, meaning "hall for considering politics" is a building used as the main executive office by the king. Located behind Geunjeongjeon Hall, the king carried out his executive duties and held meetings with the top government officials. Two separate side buildings, Cheonchujeon and Manchunjeon, flank the west and east of Sajeongjeon, and while Sajeongjeon is not equipped with a heating system, these buildings are equipped with *ondols* 온돌 (underfloor heating that uses direct heat transfer from wood smoke to heat the underside of a thick masonry floor) for their use in the colder months.

천추전 Cheonchujeon

수정전 Sujeongjeon

Meaning "hall for proper management of the state affairs", is a building located to the south of Gyeonghoeru 경회루, was constructed in 1867 and used by the cabinet of the Joseon dynasty.

강녕전 Gangnyeongjeon

Gangnyeongjeon is a building used as the king's main residing quarters. First constructed in 1395, the fourth year of King Taejo 태조, the building contains the king's bed chamber. Destroyed during the Japanese invasions of Korea in 1592, the building was rebuilt when Gyeongbokgung was reconstructed in 1867, but it was again burned down by a major fire in November 1876 and had to be restored in 1888 following the orders of King Gojong 고종.

However, when Huijeongdang 희정당 of Changdeokgung Palace was burned down by a fire in 1917, the Japanese government dismembered the building and used its construction materials to restore Huijeongdang in 1920. Current Gangnyeongjeon was built in 1994, meticulously restoring the building to its original specifications and design.

It consists of corridors and fourteen rectangular chambers, each seven chambers located to the left and right side of the building in a layout out like a checkerboard. The king used the central chamber while the court attendants occupied the remaining side chambers to protect, assist, and to receive orders. The building rests on top of a tall stone foundation, and a stone deck or veranda is located in front of the building.

The noted feature of the building is an absence of a top white roof ridge called *yongmaru* 용마루 in Korean. Many theories exist to explain the absence, of which a prominent one states that, since the king was symbolized as the dragon during the Joseon Dynasty, the *yongmaru*, which contains the letter dragon or *yong*, cannot rest on top of the king when he is asleep.

교태전 Gyotaejeon

Gyotaejeon, also called Gyotaejeon Hall, is a building used as the main residing quarters by the queen during the Joseon Dynasty. It's located behind Gangnyeongjeon, the king's quarters, and contains the queen's bed chamber. It was first constructed in around 1440, the 22nd year of King Sejong the Great 세종대왕.

King Sejong, who was noted to have frail health later in his reign, decided to carry out his executive duties in Gangnyeongjeon, where his bed chamber is located, instead of Sajeongjeon. Since this decision meant many government officials routinely needed to visit and intrude Gangnyeongjeon, King Sejong had Gyotaejeon built in consideration of his wife the queen's privacy.

The building was burned down in 1592 when the Japanese invaded Korea, but was reconstructed in 1867. Nevertheless, when Daejojeon 대조전 of Changdeokgung Palace 창덕궁 was burned down by a fire in 1917, the Japanese government disassembled the building and recycled its construction materials to restore Daejojeon. The current building was reconstructed in 1994 according to its original design and specifications. The building, like Gangnyeongjeon, does not have a top roof ridge called yongmaru.

Amisan 아미산, a famous garden created from an artificial mound, is located behind Gyotaejeon. Four hexagonal chimneys, constructed around 1869 in orange bricks and decorative roof tiles, adorn Amisan without showing their utilitarian function and are notable examples of formative art created during the Joseon Dynasty. The chimneys were registered as Korea's Treasure No. 811 on January 8, 1985.

자경전 Jagyeongjeon

Jagyeongjeon, is a building used as the main residing quarters by Queen Sinjeong 신정왕후, the mother of King Heonjong 헌종. First constructed in 1865, it was burned down twice by a fire but was reconstructed in 1888. Jagyeongjeon is the only royal residing quarters in Gyeongbokgung that survived the demolition campaigns of the Japanese government during the Japanese occupation of Korea.

The chimneys of Jagyeongjeon are decorated with ten signs of longevity to wish for a long life for the late queen, while the west walls of the Jagyeongjeon compound are adorned with floral designs. The protruding southeast part of Jagyeongjeon, named Cheongyeollu 청연루, is designed to provide a cooler space during the summer, while the northwest part of Jagyeongjeon, named Bokandang 복안 당, is designed for the winter months. The eastern part of Jagyeogjeon, named Hyeopgyeongdang and distinguished by the building's lower height, was used by the late queen's assistants.

The building and the decorative walls were registered as Korea's Treasure No. 809 on January 8, 1985.

건천궁 Geoncheongung

Also known as Geoncheonggung Residence, was a private royal residence built by King Gojong 고종within the palace grounds in 1873.

King Gojong resided in Geoncheonggung from 1888 and the residence was continuously expanded, but on October 8, 1895, Empress Myeongseong 명성황후, the wife of King Gojong, was brutally assassinated by the Japanese agents at the residence. Her body was burned and buried near the residence.

Haunted by the experiences of the incident, the king left the palace in January 1896 and never again returned to the residence. Demolished completely by the Japanese government in 1909, the residence was accurately reconstructed to its former design and open to the public in 2007.

집옥재
Jibokjae

Located next to Geoncheonggung Residence, is a two-story private library used by King Gojong. In 1876, a major fire occurred in Gyeongbokgung Palace, and King Gojong, for a brief period, moved and resided in Changdeokgung Palace. He eventually moved back to Gyeongbokgung in 1888, but he had the pre-existing Jibokjae building disassembled and moved from Changdeokgung to the present location in 1891. Its name, Jibokjae, translates loosely in English as the "hall of collecting jade".

The building uniquely shows the heavy influence of Chinese architecture instead of traditional Korean palace architecture. Its side walls were entirely constructed in brick, a method commonly employed by the contemporary Chinese, and its roof formations, interior screens, and columns also show Chinese influences. Its architecture possibly was meant to give it an exotic appearance.

It's flanked by Parujeong 팔우정, an octagonal two-story pavilion, to the left and Hyeopgildang 협길당 to the right. Parujeong was constructed to store books, while Hyeopgildang served as a part of Jibokjae. Both of the buildings are internally connected to Jibokjae. Bohyeondang 보현당 and Gahoejeong 가회정, buildings that also formed a library complex to the south of Jibokjae, were demolished by the Japanese government in the early 20th century.

40

동궁 Donggung

Donggung, located south of the Hyangwonjeong pavilion 향원정, was the living quarters for the crown prince and his wife. The four main buildings of the compound were Jaseondang 자선당 and Bihyeongak 비현각, Chunbang 춘방 (the lecture hall, where the prince received the preparatory education in order to become a future monarch), as well as Gyebang 계방 (the security building). In the 19th century, the future Emperor Sunjong 순종황제 lived in the compound. Donggung was razed to the ground during the Japanese occupation. The restoration work started in 1999, and currently, only Jaseondang and Bihyeongak were restored.

Gyeonghoeru, also known as Gyeonghoeru Pavilion, is a hall used to hold important and special state banquets during the Joseon Dynasty. It is registered as Korea's National Treasure No. 224 on January 8, 1985.

The first Gyeonghoeru was constructed in 1412, the 12th year of the reign of King Taejong, but was burned down during the Japanese invasions of Korea in 1592. The present building was constructed in 1867 (the 4th year of the reign of King Gojong) on an island of an artificial, rectangular lake that is 128 m wide and 113 m across.

Constructed mainly of wood and stone, it has a form where the wooden structure of the building sits on top of 48 massive stone pillars, with wooden stairs connecting the second floor to the first floor. The outer perimeters are supported by square pillars while the inner columns are cylindrical; they were placed thus to represent the idea of Yin & Yang.

When it was originally built in 1412, these stone pillars were decorated with sculptures depicting dragons rising to the sky, but these details were not reproduced when the building was rebuilt in the 19th century. Three stone bridges connect the building to the palace grounds, and corners of the balustrades around the island are decorated with sculptures depicting twelve Zodiac animals.

경회루 Gyeonghoeru

향원정 Hyangwonjeong

Hyangwonjeong, is a small, two-story hexagonal pavilion built around 1873 by the order of King Gojong when Geoncheonggung residence was built to the north within Gyeongbokgung.

The pavilion was constructed on an artificial island of a lake named Hyangwonji 향원지 , and a bridge named Chwihyanggyo 취향교 connects it to the palace grounds. The name Hyangwonjeong is loosely translated as "pavilion of far-reaching fragrance", while Chwihyanggyo is "bidge intoxicated with fragrance".

The bridge Chwihyanggyo was originally located on the north side of the island and was the longest bridge constructed purely of wood during the Joseon Dynasty; however, it was destroyed during the Korean War. The bridge was reconstructed in its present form on the south side of the island in 1953, but is now being relocated to its original location on the north side.

잡상 Japsang

The roofs are made of clay tiles, *giwa* 기와 and are decorated with figurines called *japsang*. There is always an odd number of the smaller *japsang*. The most a building can have is 11. The purpose of the roof decorations goes back to the Korean shamanic religion and they are intended to chase away evil spirits and misfortune as well as show the dignity and grandeur of a building. The first few japsang on a roof are usually characters from the Chinese classic Journey to the West. The types of *japsang* are:

Dragon's Head (*Yong-du*)
Eagle's Head (*Chwui-du*)
Owl's Tail (*Chi-mi*)
Buddhist Monk (*Daedangsabu*)
Monkey King (*Sonhaengja*)
Friar Sand "Sandy" (*Sahwasang*)
Honred Beast (*Igwibak*)
Two-Mouhted Dragon (*Iguryong*)
Horse (*Mahwasang*)
Bodhisattva (*Samsalbosal*)
Pangolin (*Cheonsangap*)
Animal-Looking Ghost (*Natodu*)

십장생 Shipjangsaeng

Shipjangsaeng, meaning "ten 10 traditional symbols of longevity", are a traditional Korean pattern. The pattern will arrange similar symbols to strengthen the original meaning of the symbol. The ten symbols include: sun, mountain, rock, water, cloud, pine tree, elixir plant, turtle, crane, and deer.

Each symbol in the pattern stands for longevity, but when used together it strengthens their original meaning. The number ten (ship) also represents completeness.

장독대 Jangdokdae

Jangdokdae is an outside space, most frequently a terrace, where a series of jars are gathered. The jars are a subkind of *jangdok* (or *onggi* 옹기), a Korean ethnic earthenware. They are used to ferment or simply store comestible goods, typically *kimchi*, soybeans, bean and red pepper paste or grains. *Jangdok* means "crock" (for condiments and soy sauce) and dae means "place", "support". *Jangdokdae* means "place for *jangdok*(s)". The jars are called *hangari* 항아리 or *onggi*.

This place is commonly found directly near traditional Korean houses, more precisely near the kitchen. Sunshine and ventilation are key aspects in the location choice, so that foods can be preserved and kept fresh. Well-preserved ingredients may stay for several years in the jars. The similar terraces of royal palaces were called *yeomgo* 염고 and were supervised by a court lady, called *janggo mama* 장고마마.

이순신 장군 동상
Statue of Admiral Yi Sun-sin

The statue of Admiral Yi Sun-sin is located at the Sejong-no, Gwanghwamun Plaza in Seoul, South Korea. It is dedicated to the 16th-century Korean war hero, admiral Yi Sun-sin. Standing 17 meters tall and made from bronze, ot depicts a standing figure of the admiral, who is holding a sword in his right hand. A miniature turtle ship, or *geobukseon* 거북선, a type of contemporary Korean war vessel commanded by Yi Sun-sin, is also located in front of the statue. Two models of war drums are also present near the statue.

This statue was erected on 27 April 1968 in the presence of the presidential pair. It was designed by Kim Se-jung (1928–1986), a sculptor and professor of art at Seoul National University, aided by the historians from the National Institute of Korean History. It was the first statue built by the Statue Establishing Committee led by Kim Jong-pil, who was asked by President Park Chung Hee: "Build a statue of a person most feared and admired by the Japanese in the Sejong-no intersection." The raising of the statue, also a part of a renovation of the Gwanghwamun Plaza, was one of the symbols of modernization and rebuilding of Korea. The armored figure of the war hero has also been considered a symbol of the then-military government of South Korea. At the time of its unveiling, it was the tallest standing statue in Asia.

In 2005, the South Korean government considered moving a statue to another location, but after a public debate, the plans were canceled. In November 2010, the statue was removed for 40 days to undergo restoration works. Moving for the first time in 42 years, it was lifted by a 200-ton crane and transported to a factory in Icheon, Gyeonggi Province. It underwent sand-blasting to remove rust, accumulated grime such as from roadside pollution; and repainted before returning to the Plaza. Other works included fortifying the inner skeleton and the restored statue was unveiled to the public on 23 December 2010. During the time the statue was being renovated, it was replaced by 3 m long, 3 m wide and 6 m high rectangular column displaying life-size photos of the statue. Throughout its four decades, the statue color has changed from bronze to deep green hue and it was decided the renovated statue would be a mix of both colors. During the renovation, Korean public and historians also debated whether his face, sword or armor (the last two criticized by some for being too Chinese or Japanese, and not enough Korean) are accurately represented.

Next to the statue, there is also a water fountain in honor of the achievements of Admiral Yi Sun-sin. It is named the 12.23 Fountain, to commemorate the 23 battles he fought with 12 warships when he led Koreans to victory during the Japanese invasions of Korea. The water jets rises to a height of 18 meters along with 300 smaller jets, which symbolize the battles he fought on the sea. A small museum is located underneath the statue.

Admiral Yi Sun-sin statue is located 250 meters from the other large statue on the Plaza, the statue of King Sejong.

세종대왕 동상
Statue of
King Sejong The Great

Statue of King Sejong is located at the Sejong-no, Gwanghwamun Plaza in central Seoul, South Korea. It is dedicated to the 15th-century Korean monarch, Sejong the Great, the fourth king of Joseon dynasty and one of Korea's most famous historical figures. The statue is considered one of Seoul's major landmarks. Unveiled in 2009, it has been called "South Korea's most iconic statue."

The statue was constructed as part of the creation of new public space in central Seoul, the Gwanghwamun Plaza, located next to the Gyeongbokgung Palace complex. The statue of King Sejong was designed by Kim Yeong-won, a carving and modeling professor at Hongik University. Early plans for the Gwanghwamun Plaza included moving the statue of King Sejong from Deoksugung palace complex to the Gwanghwamun Plaza. However, after public discussions involving surveys of citizens and experts, it was decided to commission a new statue of King Sejong. Its design was chosen after a competition between a shortlist of artists recommended by the Korean Fine Arts Association and universities. The new statue was designed to be sitting, unlike the nearby older standing statue of Admiral Yi Sun-sin. King Sejong statue is located 250 meters from the other large statue on the Gwanghwamun Plaza, the statue of the Admiral Yi Sun-sin.

The statue of King Sejong was dedicated on 9 October 2009, in a ceremony attended by President Lee Myung-bak and other Korean government officials, on a *Hangul* Day 한글날 in celebration of the 563rd anniversary of the invention of the Korean alphabet by King Sejong, two months after the Gwanghwamun Plaza opening. The golden statue is 6.2 meters high and weighs 20 tons. The king has one hand raised and another placed on a book. Sides of the statue display all of the hangul alphabet characters. In front of the statue, there are small models of a celestial globe, a rain gauge, and a sundial, the invention of which is also traditionally attributed to King Sejong in Korea.

While King Sejong is best remembered for his invention of hangul, he is also considered to have been involved in the promotion of agriculture, literature, science and technology, as well as Confucian philosophy, in Korea.

Near the statue, a 'Sejong's Story' an exhibition hall, a small museum dedicated to King Sejong, can be found.

창덕궁 Changdeokgung

Meaning "prospering virtue palace", it was the second palace after Gyeongbokgung which had been established in 1395 as a primary palace. Due to its location, east of Gyeongbokgung, Changdeokgung—along with Changgyeonggung— it's also referred to as the "east palace", or Donggwol 동궐.

Changdeokgung was the most favored palace of many Joseon princes and retained many elements dating from the Three Kingdoms of Korea period that were not incorporated in the more contemporary Gyeongbokgung. One such element is the fact that the buildings blend with the natural topography of the site instead of imposing themselves upon it.

Amid strife for the throne between princes and vassals, the authority of Gyeongbokgung was deteriorated. King Jeongjong enthroned by Prince Jeong-an 정안공 (Yi Bang-won 이방원, later became King Taejong 태종) moved the capital to Gaegyeong, 개경 the one of Goryeo Dynasty, again in 1400 on the pretext of superior geographical features of it, in fact, in order to avert the power struggle. King Taejong soon taking over the throne returned to Hanseong 한성 (present-day Seoul) had a new palace named Changdeokgung instead of Gyeongbokgung because he had killed his half brothers in Gyeongbokgung whose construction was led by Jeong Do-jeon, the king's rival before. Construction of Changdeok Palace began in 1405 and was completed in 1412. King Seonjo 인조 expanded the palace grounds by about 500,000 square meters, including Huwon 후원.

The Palace was burnt to the ground during the Japanese invasion in 1592 and reconstructed in 1609 by King Seonjo 인조 and King Gwanghaegun 광해군. The palace burnt down again in 1623 because of King Injo 인조 a political Revolt against Gwanghaegun. The palace was also attacked by the Manchu Qing but throughout its history of reconstruction and repair has remained faithful to its original design. Changdeokgung was the site of the royal court and the seat of government until 1868 when the neighboring Gyeongbokgung was rebuilt. Korea's last Emperor, Sunjong 순종황제 lived here until his death in 1926. Other members of the former Royal family were permitted to live in parts of the palace such as former Crown Prince Yi Un 이은 who lived in the Nakseon-jae (hall) Buildings with his wife Princess Bangja and sister Princess Deokhye until their respective deaths; this arrangement was periodically interrupted by differing Presidential orders supporting and objecting to their use of the historic facilities. The son of Yi-Un, Yi-Gu 이구 also lived in the Palace for variant intervals prior to moving to a semi-permanent residence in Tokyo due to mental health issues having been unable to fully adapt to the new Korea.

Today there are 13 buildings remaining on the palace grounds and 28 pavilions in the gardens, occupying 110 acres (45 hectares) in all and the area is designated as Historical Site No. 122. Buildings of note include Donhwamun 돈화문 (built in 1412, rebuilt in 1607, with a copper bell weighing 9 short tons or 8 metric tons), Injeongjeon 인정전 (main hall), Seonjeongjeon 선정전 (auxiliary office in the main hall), Huijeongdang 희정당 (the king's private residence, later used as a conference hall), Daejojeon 대조전 (living quarters), and Nakseon-jae.

King's houses like Seonjeongjeon, Huijeongdang, and Nakseonjae are surrounded in many folds of buildings and courts in case of any outsider breakthrough. The overall architectural style features simplicity and frugality because of Confucian ideology.

돈화문
Donhwamun Gate

The main palace gate. Built in 1412, Donhwamun has a two-story pavilion-type wooden structure and is the largest of all palace gates. Donhwamun was burned down during the Japanese invasion of 1592 and was restored in 1608.

금천교
Geumcheongyo

All Korean royal palaces had a stream flowing through the palace grounds with a stone bridge crossing the stream.

Goblins, or *dokkaebi* 도깨비 were made into statues and engraved into the stone bridges, as the goblins and other menacing figures were believed to ward off the evil spirits, protecting the palace.

인정전 Injeongjeon

Meaning "hall of benevolent ruling", Injeongjeon was the throne hall of Changdeokgung.

It was the most representative and dignified building of the palace, used for major state affairs including the coronation of a new king and receiving foreign envoys.

Originally built in 1405, it was rebuilt in 1610 after being burned down during the 1592 Japanese invasion, and a third time in 1804 after being destroyed by a fire.

It's Korea's National Treasure No. 225.

어좌 Eojwa

Royal Throne Inside Injeongjeon

인정문 Injeongmun Gate

선정전 Seonjeongjeon

Meaning "hall of administering governance", Seonjeongjeon was an office for ruling officials. The king held daily meetings with ministers, attended to his duties and discussed state affairs and held seminars here.

The current building was constructed in 1647 and is the only remaining building with a blue-tiled roof within the palace.

희정당 Huijeongdang

Meaning "hall of joyful ruling", Huijeongdang was the king's bed chamber. It became his workplace after Seonjeongjeon, where the ancestral tablets of the deceased kings and queens were kept, was deemed too small for conducting routine state affairs. The original Huijeongdang was destroyed by a fire in 1917 but was reconstructed in 1920 with materials taken from the royal bedchamber at Gyeongbokgung. The reconstructed structure is completely different from the original due to recent Western influences. Wooden floorboards and carpets, glass windows, and chandeliers can be seen inside the building.

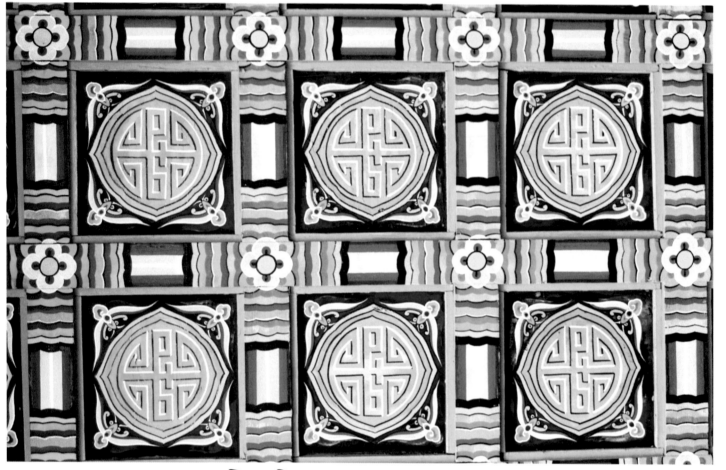

단청 Dancheong

Dancheong refers to Korean traditional decorative coloring on wooden buildings and artifacts for the purpose of style. It means "cinnabar and blue-green" in Korean. It is based on five basic colors; blue (east), white (west), red (south), black (north), and yellow (center). Dancheong has various symbolic meanings. *Dancheong* also represented social status and rank by using various patterns and colors.

It functions not only as decoration but also for practical purposes such as to protect building surfaces against temperature and to make the crudeness of materials less conspicuous. Applying *dancheong* on the surfaces of buildings require trained skills, and artisans called *dancheongjang* 단청장 designed the painted patterns.

In the 12th century a document titled Goryeo Dokyung 고려도경 which means "Illustrated Account of Goryeo" (918-1392), the Chinese author Xu Jing described the luxurious dancheong on the places at that time. It illustrates the dancheong in detail that the handrail was painted in red and decorated with vine-flowers. The coloring and patterns were very vivid so that the palace stood out among other royal palaces. There are several examples of the dancheong from the Goryeo period such as Josadang 조사당 of Buseoksa Temple 부석사 in Yeongju 영주, Geukrakjeon 극락전 at Bongjeongsa Temple 봉정사 in Andong 안동, and Daeungjeon 대웅전 of Sudeoksa Temple 수덕사 in Yesan 예산.

대조전 Daejojeon

Meaning "hall of great creation", it was the official residence of the queen, with the center of the building used as a living room and bed chambers on each side. Behind the hall was a beautifully terraced flower garden.

Destroyed by fire in 1917, it was rebuilt with materials taken from Gyotaejeon of Gyeongbokgung. Similar to Huijeongdang, the interior shows Western-style. It was used as a residence for the last empress of Joseon, allowing us a glimpse into the final years of the royal household of the Joseon Dynasty.

Backyard of Daejeongjeon

연춘문 Yeochunmun

Interior of Daejojeon

Small Garden In The Backyard

성정각 Seongjeonggak

It was an area dedicated to the crown prince, and buildings related to him are often called the Donggung 동궁, or "east palace" because they were located east side of the palace. as the crown prince was regarded as the sun just before its rise, to become the king. Seongjeonggak was the study room of the crown prince, where he studied Confucian principles, which were the backbone ideology of the Joseon dynasty.

낙선재
Nakseonjae

The Nakseonjae Complex, built in 1847 during the King Heonjong 헌종's reign was a residential compound. As Queen Myeongheon 명헌 was unable to bear a child for the king, King Heonjong took a concubine, Gyeongbin 경빈 to bear his child. Nakseonjae was constructed for her in an isolated corner inside Changdeokgung. Seokbokheon 석복헌 was the name of the residential building.

There is a pavilion, which served as a library for the king where he would read and paint. Sugangjae 수강재 was built for Queen Sunwon 순원, the grandmother of Heonjong.

In the rear of the residence is a beautiful garden, situated adjacent to a simple and elegant pavilion known as Sangryangjeong 상량정. It was used for rest as it offered a beautiful view of the palace area below. The pavilion was used by the royal family until the late 20th century. The complex was made available to the public for the first time in 2006 after many years of restoration.

후원
Huwon

Behind the palace lies the 78-acre (32 ha) Huwon ("rear garden") which was originally constructed for the use of the royal family and palace women. The garden incorporates a lotus pond, pavilions, and landscaped lawns, trees, and flowers. There are over 26,000 specimens of a hundred different species of trees in the garden and some of the trees behind the palace are over 300 years old. The garden for the private use of the king had been called 'Geumwon' ("forbidden garden") because even high officials were not allowed to enter without the king's permission. It had also been called 'Naewon' 내원 ("Inner Garden"). Today Koreans often call it 'Biwon' 비원 ("secret garden") which derived from the office of the same name in the late 19th century. Though the garden had many other names, the one most frequently used through Joseon dynasty period was 'Huwon'.

In September 2012, the Buyongjeong pavilion 부용정 in the garden was re-opened after a year-long restoration project. The pavilion was restored based on the Donggwoldo from 1820, National Treasures of South Korea No. 249.

A variety of ceremonies hosted by the king were held in Huwon. In the early period of the Joseon Dynasty, military inspections in which the king participated were often held here. King Sejo had troops parade and array before him or commanded them by himself in the garden. Also, feasts were given, archery tournaments held, and fireworks enjoyed in Huwon.

The Ongnyucheon 옥류천 ("jade stream") area is of particular interest. It contains a U-shaped water channel carved in 1636 for floating wine cups, with a small waterfall and an inscribed poem on the boulder above it. The area also contains five small pavilions.

부용지
Buyongji

주합루
Juhamnu Pavilion

Eosumun Gate 어수문 (above) leading to the Juhamnu Pavilion 주합루 (below), a two-story pavilion that served as a library and reading room during the reign of King Jeongjo 정조.

Buyongjeong 부용정 (above) a pavilion with a cross-shaped roof and two supporting pillars, where King Jeongjo and his courtiers enjoyed fishing. Jondeokjeong 존덕정 (below) is a hexagonal, two-story roof pavilion. The underside of the roof has two dragons playing with a wish-fulfilling jewel, or *yeouiju* 여의주.

Sangryangjeong 상량전, meaning "climbing up to a cool place" whose original name was Pyeongwonru 평원루, which meant "maintaining good diplomatic relations with foreign countries", and it represented the Dynasty's will to establish good relations with the various Western countries Joseon encountered during the 19th century. The name changed during the Japanese occupation.

The Ongnyucheon 옥류천 ("Jade Stream") contains a U-shaped water channel carved in 1636 for floating wine cups, with a small waterfall and an inscribed poem on the boulder above it. The area also contains five small pavilions.

The back area of Yeongyeongdang **연경당**, a residence built deep in the secret garden.
The shrine on the left is Nongsujeong **농수정**, and the wall on the right is the back of Seonhyangjae **선향재**.

펌우사 Pyeomusa Pavilion, famous for where crown prince Hyomyeong used to read and philosophize.

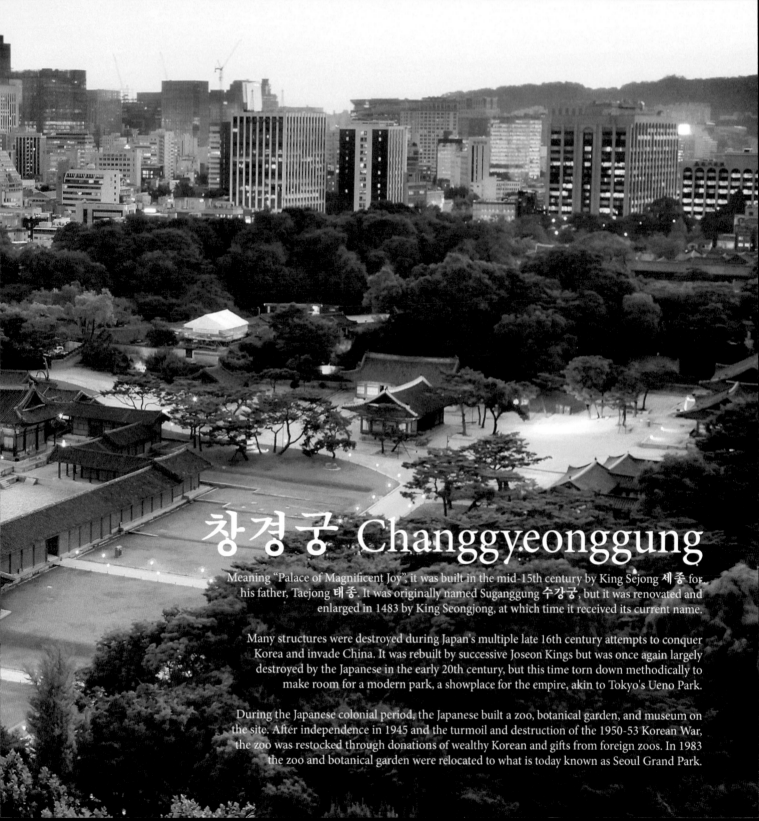

창경궁 Changgyeonggung

Meaning "Palace of Magnificent Joy", it was built in the mid-15th century by King Sejong 세종 for his father, Taejong 태종. It was originally named Suganggung 수강궁, but it was renovated and enlarged in 1483 by King Seongjong, at which time it received its current name.

Many structures were destroyed during Japan's multiple late 16th century attempts to conquer Korea and invade China. It was rebuilt by successive Joseon Kings but was once again largely destroyed by the Japanese in the early 20th century, but this time torn down methodically to make room for a modern park, a showplace for the empire, akin to Tokyo's Ueno Park.

During the Japanese colonial period, the Japanese built a zoo, botanical garden, and museum on the site. After independence in 1945 and the turmoil and destruction of the 1950-53 Korean War, the zoo was restocked through donations of wealthy Korean and gifts from foreign zoos. In 1983 the zoo and botanical garden were relocated to what is today known as Seoul Grand Park.

홍화문 Honghwamun

The palace's main gate, meaning "the gate of promoting harmony" faces eastward like the central part of the palace. First built in 1484, it burned down during the Japanese invasion of 1592 and was rebuilt in 1616.

A ball pavilion (*sipjagak* 십자각) was built on either side of this two-tiered wooden gate. Honghwamun is designated as National Treasure 384.

명정문 Myeongjeongmun

As you pass through the Honghwamun, Okcheongyo Bridge 옥천교 comes into view. Between the arches under the bridge's parapet are carved goblins (*dokkaebi* 도깨비) that are intended to ward off evil spirits. Okcheongyo Bridge was built approximately 500 years ago and serves as a symbolic entry to the courtyard.

명정전 Myeongjeonjeon

Myeongjeongjeon is the main hall of the palace, where state affairs such as meetings with officials and royal banquets were held. First built in 1484, it was burned down during the Japanese invasion of 1592.

Rebuilt in 1616, it is the oldest main hall of all the palaces in Seoul. It is smaller than the two-story main halls of Gyeongbokgung and Changdeokgung because it was originally built as living quarters, especially for dowager queens, rather than as a throne hall.

Although it is a simple, one-story structure, Myeongjeongjeon was built on an elevated stone yard that imbued it with the dignity of the main hall. Running through the courtyard in front is a three-level walkway whose center path was for the king's use only.

Surrounding the entire area is a wall-like structure of single-room units which were used by the royal guards or for royal funerals. Myeongjeongjeon is designated as National Treasure 226.

The Royal Throne, *eojwa* 어좌, inside Myeongjeongjeon.

The roof viewed from the Royal Throne.

문정전 Munjeongjeon

Munjeongjeon is a council hall where the king dealt with routine state affairs. Unlike the throne hall, which faces east, this building faces south. Such a palace layout with a secondary structure facing a different direction than a throne hall is highly unusual in Korea. Munjeongjeon was also used to enshrine royal tablets after funerals.

It was dismantled during the Japanese occupation, but was restored in 1986 along with Munjeongmun Gate and the eastern part of the roofed corridor.

According to the nineteenth-century *donggwoldo* 동궐도 "painting of the east palace", Munjeongjeon was partitioned from Sungmundang and Myeongjeongjeon by a wall, and had a small annex; the courtyard was surrounded by a wall-like corridor. This part has not yet been restored.

107

Meaning "revering writing/literature", Sungmundang Hall, was where the king threw banquets to discuss state affairs and classical literature. It is believed to have been built under King Gwanghaegun 광해군 when Changgyeonggung was first rebuilt.

숭문당 Sungmundang

Burned down in 1830, it was rebuilt in autumn of the same year. Its foundation was designed to make the hall appear elevated on the sloped ground; the base stones for the front columns were made high, while those in the rear were made low. The name of the building "Sungmundang" written by King Yeongjo 영조 still hangs at the entrance.

빈양문 Binyangmun

Meaning "respectfully greeting the brightness (or the King)", Binyangmun Gate connects the King's official space and private quarters, and for this reason, access through this gate was strictly prohibited. The current building was rebuilt in 1986 after destruction during the Japanese occupation period.

함인정 Haminjeong

Meaning "the whole world is soaked with the benevolence and virtue of the king," Haminjeong was first built in 1633 on the former site of Inyangjeon Hall 인양전, and was destroyed by fire in 1830 and rebuilt in 1833. The king used this pavilion to receive officials and hold banquets. Haminjeong today is open on all four sides, but as depicted in *donggwoldo* 동궐도 "painting of the east palace", it had walls on three sides.

The signboard of Haminjeong

The view of the roof from below

경춘전 Gyeongchunjeon

Rebuilt in 1834, Gyeongchunjeon was the sleeping quarters of the wife of the deceased king. The building originally had a separate area surrounded by *haenggak* 행각 (a roofed, wall-like structure whose interior was used as shelter for low-ranking palace workers or for storage). Gyeongchunjeon was also used as a delivery room, and this is where many kings of the Joseon Dynasty were born, including King Jeongjo 정조 and King Heonjong 헌종. To commemorate his own birth, King Jeongjo himself wrote a plaque meaning "Birth Hall" and hung it above the entrance.

환경전 Hwangyeongjeon

Hwangyeongjeon Hall was a residence or council hall used by some Joseon kings. This is where King Yeongjo 영조 (r. 1724-1776) ordered his son Crown Prince Sado 사도세자 (1735-1762) to serve as a regent in 1749. The prince, then just a fifteen-year-old boy, asked the king to withdraw the order but had to suffer a harsh learning period instead. It was also here that King Jungjong 중종 (r. 1506-1544) had his disease cured by a famous female royal practitioner Dae Jang-geum 대장금, who, according to the Veritable Records Sillok 실록, worked for his queen consort and queen mother, and received a prize from the king for her devotion and achievement.

통명전 Tongmyeongjeon

It was the official residence for the queen consorts of the Joseon Dynasty, and is most famously associated with the story of Huibin Jang 장희빈 (?-1701), one of the King Sukjong's 숙종 secondary royal wives, who devised an evil scheme to expel the rightful occupant of the building, Queen Inhyeon 인현왕후 (1667-1701), from the palace so she could become the principal queen consort. Following the superstitious beliefs, she buried rats and dead birds under a stone step in front of the building, putting on a curse. Her plan worked but eventually got disclosed to the king, who ordered to poison her as a death penalty. This was such a significant event in history, to the point where King Sukjong had to make a law specifically banning the promotion of secondary royal wives to the principal queenship.

The interior of Tongmyeongjeon (above)

Yeonji 연지, the lotus pond (right, above)

Yeolcheon well 연천 (right, below)

양화당 Yanghwadang

Standing east of Tongmyeongjeon Hall, Yanghwadang was used as a residence for King Injo 인조 (r. 1623-1649) after he returned after a disgraceful surrender to Qing in 1637. While it was customary for the king to held government meetings and received Qing envoys in the throne room, King Injo instead used Yanghwadang for that purpose.

집복헌 Jipbokheon

This small residential building was where the Royal Lady Yeongbin Yi 영빈 이씨, one of the King Yeongjo's 영조 secondary wives, gave birth to a prince who would later became Crown Prince Sado 사도세자 (1735-1762), and was also a place where King Jeongjo's 정조 secondary wife, Royal Lady Subin Bak 수빈 박씨 gave birth to their son who later became King Sunjo 순조 (1800-1834). When the Crown Prince Sado was born, King Yeongjo was overwhelmed with joy, as he lost his first son just at the age of ten and had to wait seven more years to have his heir. King Yeongjo was forty years old.

영춘헌 Yeongchunheon

This small building east of Jipbokheon was used as a residence for King Jeongjo 정조 (r. 1776-1800) during his stay in Changgyeonggung. As a compassionate ruler, King Jeongjo always thought of the poverty his people had to endure during his reign, he ordered not to decorate the house and didn't mind staying in a room with a leaky ceiling. It was also in this humble place where he died, of a malignant tumor at the age of 49.

관덕정 Gwandeokjeong

This small pavilion, initially used as silkworm farms, is known to have been used as an archery field together with the wide-open space in the front which was also used for military drills by and military examination venue by soldiers. The pavilion was originally named Chwimijeong Pavilion 취미정 in 1643, but changed its name to the current one in 1664.

관천대 Gwancheondae

Meaning "sky observatory", this is an astronomical observatory built in 1688 to observe the movement of heavenly bodies via using an armillary sphere. It was managed by *Gwangsanggam* 관상감, the Meteorological Office, a government agency during the Joseon Dynasty, responsible for the observation of the movement of the sun, moon, and stars. They kept track of the changes of time according to the change of seasons, and the twenty-four solar terms and the information gathered was productively exploited by the farmers.

태실 Taesil

Taesil, meaning "placenta chamber", is located in Changgyeonggung was built to enshrine the umbilical cord and the placenta of King Seongjong 성종 (r. 1469-1494), it was because of the tradition and belief of the Joseon Dynasty that the act of storing the placentas of the royal heirs at the auspicious sites across the country under a belief that they were directly connected with the destiny of the dynasty.

This taesil at Changgyeonggung is considered the most beautiful of all the remaining ones, and was originally in Gwangju 광주 of Gyeonggi-do 경기도 but moved to the current location where Yi Royal Household Museum was set up during the Japanese colonial period (1910-1945).

앙부일구 Angbuilgu

Meaning "sundial in the shape of upturned cauldron'", this sundial was first made in 1434 during the King Sejong's 세종 reign and is designed to indicate the local apparent solar time and the twenty-four solar terms, and is considered one of the most outstanding scientific achievements of the time.

This one, currently located in the precincts of Changgyeonggung is a replica of the original now designated as the Treasure No. 845.

춘당지 Chundangji

There are two ponds called by the same name Chundangji ("Spring Pond") of which the smaller one at the back is the original Chundangji which existed since the Joseon Dynasty. The larger pond in the front had been a field called *naenongpo* 내농포, or "Inner Field", containing eleven paddies where the Joseon kings living in Changgyeonggung tilled the soil with plows drawn by an ox, wishing for a good harvest.

The field and the ceremony were an important part of the tradition, as they were a means to show an example for their people, promote farming, and share the arduous labor farmers had to endure.

Palgak Chilcheung Seoktap **팔각칠층석탑**(Above)

This occtagonal seven-story stone pagoda is known to have been purchased from a merchant, who delivered it from Manchuria and placed here next to Chundangji Pond when Yi-Royal Family Museum was built during the Japanese colonial period. This Tibetan-style pagoda contains an inscription on its body indicating that it was erected in 1470 during the Chinese Ming Dynasty.

Punggidae **풍기대** (Right)

It's a measuring instrument made of stone used to detect the velocity of wind and the direction it is blowing. It's decorated with scroll designs which are believed to have been constructed sometime in the 18th century. To use the instrument, a pole would be inserted into a hole at the top of the stone, and a piece of cloth is attached to the end of the pole. When the wind picked up, the piece of cloth would wave in the air, indicating the velocity and direction of the wind.

덕수궁 Deoksugung

Meaning "palace of virtuous longevity", it was originally known as Gyeongungung 경운궁, it's a walled compound of palaces in Seoul that was inhabited by members of Korea's royal family during the Joseon monarchy until the annexation of Korea by Japan in 1910. It is one of the "Five Grand Palaces" built by the kings of the Joseon Dynasty. The buildings are of varying styles, including some of natural cryptomeria wood, painted wood, and stucco. Some buildings were built of stone to replicate Western palatial structures. In addition to the traditional palace buildings, there are also forested gardens, a statue of King Sejong the Great and the National Museum of Art, which holds special exhibitions.

The palace is located near City Hall Station. Deoksugung, like the other "Five Grand Palaces" in Seoul, was intentionally heavily destroyed during the Japanese colonial period. Currently, only one-third of the structures that were standing before the occupation remains. Deoksugung Palace is special among Korean palaces. It has a modern and a Western-style garden and fountain. The Changing of the Royal Guard, in front of 대한문 Daehanmun Gate, is a very popular event for many visitors. The royal guard was responsible for opening and closing the palace gate during the Joseon Dynasty. Outside of the palace is a picturesque road with a stone wall.

On the site of Deoksugung were residential buildings of descendants of the royal family, including Prince Wolsan 월산대군 (1454~1488), the older brother of King Seongjong 선종 (1469~1494), and high-ranking officials of the Joseon Dynasty. When all the palaces in the capital were destroyed by fire during the Japanese invasion of Korea in 1592, King Seonjo (1567~1608) used these residential buildings as a temporary palace. In 1611, this palace became a secondary palace named Gyeongungung When King Gwanhaegun 광해군 (1608~1623) moved to 창덕궁 Changdeokgung, which was rebuilt as the official royal residence.

From that time to the mid-nineteenth century, Gyeongungung played no important role as a palace. In 1897, King Gojong 고종 proclaimed the establishment of the Great Han Empire and became an emperor. Gyeongungung became the central palace of the Great Han Empire, and a number of new buildings befitting an imperial palace were built.

As evidence of Gojong's determination to modernize the country, some of the buildings were built in a Western-style. In the 1880s, the area around the palace was called 정릉동 Jeongneung-dong and was crowded with foreign legations and residences of missionaries, making the expansion of the premises of Gyeongungung difficult. The premises eventually surrounded the already existing American, British, and Russian legations, resulting in a very irregular layout. In 1907, the palace became the residence of the former King Gojong after he relinquished the throne. The palace was renamed Deoksungung, and its premises were reduced to make way for street widening.

After Gojong passed away, 선원전 Seonwonjeon in the northern section and 중명전 Jungmyeongjeon in the Western section of the palace were sold, reducing the premises of the palace by one-third. In 1933, all of the buildings on the palace premises, except a few central buildings and Western-style buildings, were removed. The palace was then made a park and opened to the general public. The 중화전 Junghwajeon area, the center of the palace premises, and the Western-style buildings including 정관헌 Jeonggwanheon and 석조전 Seokjojeon, remain Deoksugung was the symbolic enter of resistance in the face of several national crises, including the Japanese invasion in 1592 and the difficulties during the closing years of the so-called Great Han Empire.

대한문 Daehanmun Gate

Located in the east, this served as the main entrance of the palace after the completion of 원구단 Wongudan Altar. The original main gate was 인화문 Inhwamun, but it was moved to the west because of the nearby expansion of Taepyeong-no 태평로 Street back in 1970. The changing of the Guard Ceremony takes place here every day.

History of Changing Ceremony of the Royal Guard

The concept of the Royal Guard in the Joseon Dynasty is the same as a national defense because the royal guard used as a means to strengthen the royal authority and maintain stability. The royal guard system started first when the first gate guard was assigned when King Yejong, the 8th king of the Joseon Dynasty, came to the throne in 1469. The royal guard system was structured when the gate guard system was institutionalized and rules on managing gate guards were incorporated in *gyeongguk daejeon* 경국대전 (National Code) during the reign of King Seongjong 성종, the 9th king of the Joseon Dynasty. The changing ceremony of the royal guard in front of the Daehanmun Gate started in 1906 when the gate was designated as a main gate to the Palace.

The Order of the Changing Ceremony

Entrance of the officials and announcement of the ceremony - Delivery of the pass codes and pass code response - First drumbeat (passing the case with the keys) - Second drumbeat (checking the authenticity of the token and identification of the plate which represents the chief gatekeeper, *sumunjang* 수문장) - Third drumbeat (implementation of the shift) - Closing announcement

The *yonggo* 용고 ("dragon drum"), is a barrel drum with tacked heads decorated with painted dragon designs, used in the military wind-and-percussion music called *daechwita* 대취타. It's sometimes also classified as a *buk* 북 and is struck with two padded sticks.

Just past the Gate is Geumcheongyo Bridge 금천교, built in 1411, excavated and restored in 1986 - the oldest surviving bridge in Seoul. Entering through the gate, you will cross over a stream (a sacred pool that each royal palace had), and it symbolizes purifying yourself before entering.

광명문 | 光明門

Gwangmyeongmun Gate

Gwangmyeongmun Gate, which served as the entrance to Hamnyeongjeon
Hall, the official residence of Emperor Gojong (r. 1863~1907), was built just
after the proclamation of the Korean Empire in 1897. However, Deoksugung
Palace was seriously damaged in the colonial period (1910~1945), resulting in
the demolition of the corridors flanking Gwangmyeongmun Gate and, eventually,
relocation of the gate itself. The gate was returned to its original location in
December 2018 as part of the plan to restore Deoksugung Palace.

153

Hamnyeongjeon was the sleeping quarters of King Gojong (1852~1919). The king passed away here in 1919. Hamnyeongjeon had been destroyed by fire earlier in 1904 and rebuilt the same year. These are typical royal sleeping quarters with an *ondol* 온돌 heating system under the floor on both sides, a wooden floored room in the center and a walkaway-like servants' quarters surrounding the *ondol* rooms. Hamnyeongjeon has a terraced rear garden, Yuhyeonmun Gate 유현문, and a decorative chimney. The king received high-ranking officials and foreign envoys in Deokbongjeon. It was built as a traditional structure in 1911, however, the interior was decorated in Western-style with a chandelier suspended from the ceiling.

Hamnyeongjeon's main floor were *ondol* 온돌 rooms (floor heating rooms).
East *ondol* room was used for Emperor Gojong's bedroom and the West *ondol* room was used for his concubines' bedroom.

Deokhongjeon Hall 덕홍전 was constructed after Gyeonghyojeon 경효전, built for Queen Myeongseong's funeral ceremony after she was murdered by Japanese assassins, was relocated to Seonwonjeon's 선원전 location. It was then used as a reception place where Emperor Gojong greeted his subjects and visitors from foreign countries. In 1911, upon relocation of Gyeonghyojeon to Seonwonjeon's location, Deokhongjeon was rebuilt. Contrary to other buildings, Deokhongjeon incorporated Western styles, from lightings, curtains to the main gate. It is connected to Hamnyeongjeon by a corridor and has Western-style 'opening and closing' doors.

유현문 Yuhyeonmun

3

정관헌 | 靜觀軒
Jeonggwanheon

Situated on the hill of the rear garden looking down on the palace, this was a building for rest and entertainment, built around 1900. It has both Korean and Western features and was designed by Russian architect, A. I. Sabatin. It is surrounded by outer rows of covered colonnades made of imitation stone in a Romanesque style. Verandas were built to the east, south, and west. The columns on the verandas are made of wood. The top of these columns are decorated with carvings in traditional Korean motifs such as a blue and gold dragons, bats, and flower vases. King Gojong is said to have enjoyed coffee and held banquets for foreign envoys in this Western-style building.

Inside of Jeonggwanheon reflecting the Western-style interior.

(Above) The symbol of a deer keeping a herb of eternal youth, *bulocho* 불로초 means longing for a healthy long life.
(Left, below) Tiles of Jeonggwanheon's floor maintain their original form even after 100 years.
(Right, below) Symbols of bats were known to attract fortune and scare away ghosts as well as fertility.

준명당 Junmyeongdang

Meaning "hall of bright principles of ruling", Junmyeongdang, connected to Jeukjodang, was a newly built building when Emperor Gojong returned to Deoksugung from his escape to the Russian legation in 1897 and was used as a place to greet visitors from foreign countries.

Emperor Gojong had no connection with the outside world, had Princess Deokye 덕혜옹주 at the age of 60. He loved her so much and Junmyeongdang was used as her kindergarten.

즉조당 일원 | 卽阼堂
Jeukjodang Area

In this area are royal buildings where King Seonjo (1567-1608) stayed during the Japanese invasion of 1592. Jeukjodang, in the center, is where King Gwanghaegun and King Injo were crowned. Another historic building is Seogeodang, on the right, where King Seonjo lived and passed away. Seogeodang is a two-story wooden house. Because it is unpainted, Seogeodang looks like an ordinary home. In 1623, most of the buildings and lands were returned to their original owners, but these two buildings (Jeukjodang and Seogeodang) were preserved as symbols of the palace. Junmyeongdang, on the left, is where King Gojong (1864-1907) administered state affairs. It is connected to Jeukjodang by a corridor. Burned down in 1904, these three buildings were rebuilt the same year.

중화전 일원 | 中和殿
Junghwajeon Area

Junghwajeon, the throne hall, and the courtyard in front of it are symbolic spaces where state ceremonies were held. A broad two-tiered stone terrace paved with wide, flat stones forms the base of the throne hall. Stone markers indicate where the officials stood according to rank during royal assemblies. These rank stones and the three-lane path running through the courtyard are faithful to the norms of traditional palace architecture. The center lane of the path was reserved for the king.

Junghwajeon was built in 1902 south of Jeukjodang, which had been used as a temporary throne hall, and formed the center of the palace. Originally it was a two-story structure but it was badly damaged by fire in 1904. In 1906 it was reconstructed in its current one-story form. The cloisters surrounding the courtyard, which served as shelter for palace workers or storage space, were also rebuilt. Today only the southeast corner of the cloisters remains.

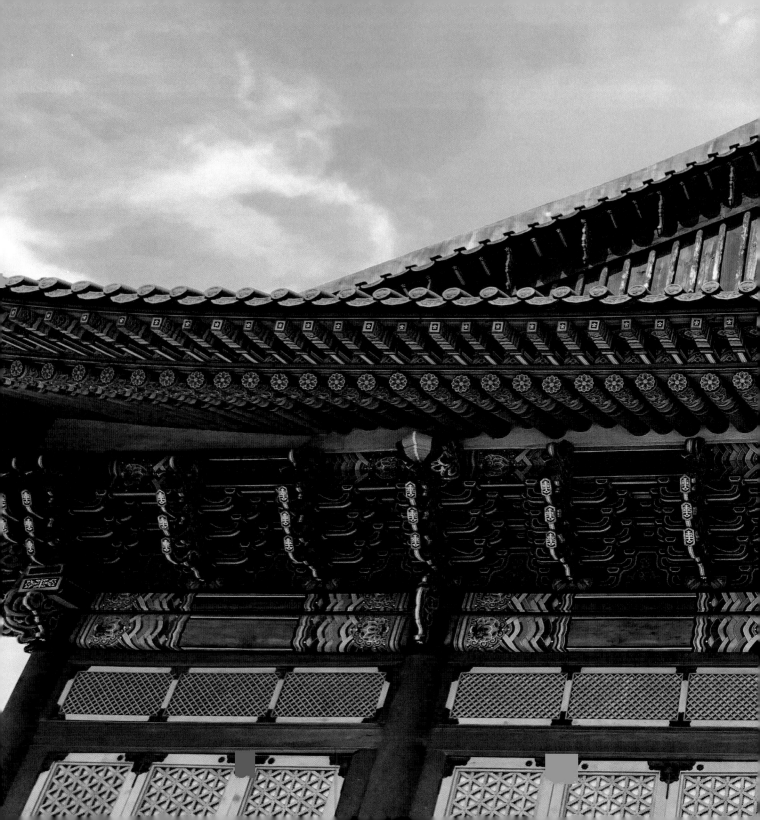

Two rows of rank stones, called *pumgyeseok* 품계석, indicate the position of court officials during ceremonies.

Seokjojeon is a Western-style building used by King Gojong as sleeping quarters and an audience hall. Designed by J.R.Harding, a British architect, construction of Seokjojeon was completed in 1910. It was built in the 19th century neoclassical style, fronted with a colonnade of the Ionic style and topped with a triangular gabled roof. Later, Seokjojeon was used as an art museum. When the west wing was expanded in 1938, a Western-style garden with a fountain was created in the front. Corinthian columns stand in front of the entrance to the west wing.

덕수궁 중명전
德壽宮 重明殿
Jungmyeongjeon Hall of Deoksugung Palace

The Jungmyeongjeon Area formerly was a residential area for Western missionaries. The area was incorporated into the palace premises when Gyeongungung Palace(today's Deoksugung Palace) was expanded in 1897. Because the American legation had already been established between here and the main buildings of Gyeongungung Palace, this area was used as a kind of separate palace.

Jungmyeongjeon Hall was built as a royal library in 1899. The hall was originally a single–story Western–style building, but it was rebuilt as a two–story building after the original was destroyed by fire in 1901.

There were at that time ten more buildings in this area, including Hwanbyeokjeong Pavilion and Manhuidang Hall, as well as Jungmyeongjeon Hall, although all but the latter disappeared during the 1920s.

Jungmyeongjeon Hall was used as a temporary residence by Emperor Gojong from 1904, when a fire broke out in the palace, to 1907 when he was dethroned by the Japanese imperialists. It was here that Korea was coerced into signing the Eulsaneukyak Treaty in 1905.

경희궁 Gyeonghuigung

Meaning "Palace of Joy and Harmony", the construction of Gyeonghuigung began in 1617 during the reign of King Gwanghaegun 광해군, the 15th king of the Joseon Dynasty, and was completed in 1620. It was originally called Gyeongdeokgung 경덕궁 because Gyeongdeok was the posthumous epithet of Wonjong 원종, who was named king after his death.

In the latter Joseon Dynasty period, Gyeonghuigung served as the secondary palace for the king, and as it was situated on the west side of Seoul, it was also called Seogwol 서궐 (a palace of the west). The Secondary palace is usually the palace where the King moves to in times of emergency.

From King Injo to King Cheoljong 철종, about ten kings of the Joseon Dynasty stayed here at Gyeonghuigung. This palace was built using the slanted geography of the surrounding mountain, has traditional beauty in its architecture and a lot of historical significance. For a time, it was of a considerable size, even to the point of having an arched bridge connecting it to Deoksugung palace. For the king's royal audience, there were the Sungjeongjeon 숭정전 and Jajeongjeon 자정전 buildings, and for sleeping, Yungbokjeon 융복전 and Hoesangjeon 회상전 buildings.

Most of Gyeonghuigung was lost to two fires that broke out in the 19th century, during the reigns of King Sunjo 순조 and King Gojong 고종. The Japanese dismantled what remained of the palace during their occupation of the Korean peninsula, to make space for Gyeongseong 경성 Middle School for Japanese citizens. Two major structures of the former palace - the Sungjeongjeon throne hall and the Heunghwamun gate 흥화문 - were disassembled and moved to other parts of Seoul. Reconstruction started in the 1990s as part of the South Korean government's initiative to rebuild the "Five Grand Palaces" that were heavily destroyed by the Japanese. However, due to urban growth and decades of neglect, the government was only able to reconstruct around 33% of the former Palace.

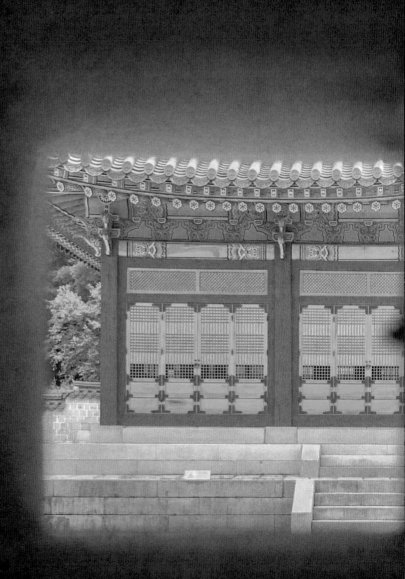

흥화문 Heunghwamun

Meaning "gate that promotes harmony", Heunghwamun was built around 1620 (12th year of King Gwanghaegun 광해군's reign) and is the front gate of Gyeonghuigung. It was relocated to the south of the palace in 1915 when a school for the Japanese was built. In 1932, it was moved to Bangmunsa 방문사, the shrine to honor Ito Hirobumi, the first Resident-General of Joseon during the Japanese occupation. where it was used as the front gate. After independence, it was used as the front gate of Yeongbingwan which was used located at the site of Bangmunsa. Later on, it was even used as the front gate of Hotel Shilla. The gate measures five kan in the front, two at the sides, and features an Ujingak 우진각 roof (hipped roof) mounted on multiple brackets. King Gwanghaegun established the palace at the foot of Inwang Mt. 인왕산, which was thought to contain the spirits of past kings. However, after Imjin War with Japan, the construction was considered to be too excessive to continue. King Gwanghaegun constructed the front door with only one story in a bid to win over the retainers insisting on the suspension of the construction. It was moved to its present location in 1988 when the Seoul Metropolitan Government initiated to the restoration of the palace. However, this is not its original location. We can find the entire grand Gyeonghuigung structure in seogwoldoan 서궐도안, the blueprint of the palace made in the 1820s. One part of the original palace, Sungjeongjeon, still remains to this day in Dongguk 동국 University.

숭정문 Sungjeongmun

Sungjeongmun was the main gate to the main hall, Sungjeongjeon. For that reason, it was the most frequently accessed gate within the palace, and it's more beautiful and magnificent than any other gates.

숭정전 Sungjeongjeon

Passed the Sungjeongmun is the main hall of Gyeonghugung, Sungjeongjeon. It means "hall of revering state affairs", which was constructed in 1618. Here, kings met with their subjects in the morning and arranged official ceremonies, such as royal feast for foreign diplomats. Gyeongjong 경종, (the 20th king), Jeongjo 정조 (the 22nd king), and Heonjong 헌종 (the 24th king) all held their inauguration ceremonies in here. The Imperial Japan dismantled Gyeonghuigung and sold the building materials to a Japanese temple in 1926, and it currently remains as Jeonggakwon temple 정각원 in Dongguk 동국 University.

Around the corners of the hall, there are bronze water jars, called deumeu 드므 or deumu 드무, with water filled up to the brim. While they serve practical purposes of putting off fire in the event of a fire, their main purpose was to ward off the evil spirits of fire - it was believed that the reflection on the water inside the jars would startle them.

During the Winter, they would keep fire around the jars to prevent them from freezing. This is a great example of harmony between shamanistic traditions and scientific reasoning of the time.

궁중생활상재현전시 - 숭정전

Exhibition on the revival of life in the palace - Sungjeongjeon

1. **오봉병** Royal Screen
2. **청선** Honor Flag (Cheongseon Fan)
3. **향좌아, 향관지** Incense support / Incense vase
4. **어좌** Royal Throne
5. **숭지 자리** Secretary's seat

6. **서안** Reading Table
7. **연상** Inkstone Table
8. **사관 자리** Historiographer's seat
9. **좌둥** Lamp
10. **일산** Honor Flag (Parasol)
11. **용선** Honor Flag (Dragon Fan)

12. **봉선** Honor Flag (Phoenix Fan)
13. **별운검** Sword (Byeol un geom)
14. **홍양산** Honor Flag (Hongyangsan)
15. **금월부** Honor Flag (Geumwolbu)
16. **수정장** Honor Flag (Sujeongjang)
17. **향로, 향합** Incense Burner, incense

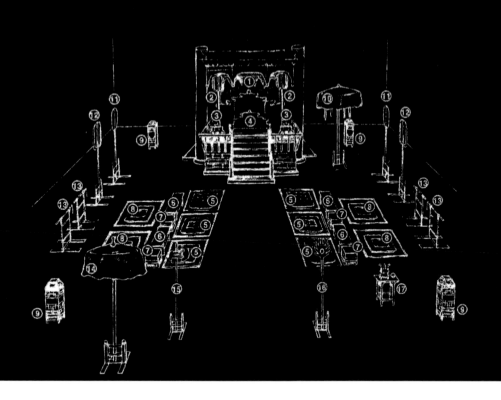

자정문 Jajeongmun

Located North of the main hall Sungjeongjeon, Jajeongmun was the main gate leading to the king's private office, Jajeongjeon, and because the path from Sungjeongjeon to Jajeongjeon is steep and narrow, the stairs are also high and steep.

자정전 Jajeonjeon

Constructed during 1617-1620, it's the king's private office. The kings held meetings with their subjects and supervised academic competitions here. When King Sukjong 숙종 died, it was used as *binjeon* 빈전 (a royal palace where the coffin of a king or queen was preserved before a funeral bier) and the *eojin* 어진 (royal portrait) or memorial tablet of late kings were temporarily preserved here, too. The Imperial Japan demolished the place and the municipal government of Seoul discovered and verified the area. The current building was restored according to the *seogwoldoan* 서궐도안, sketches for the western palaces.

태령전 Taeryeongjeon

Originally, there was no designated use for this structure. But in 1744, the 20th year of King Yeongjo's 영조 rule, a renovation was undertaken and the king's portrait was given a special place of its own.

This portrait of King Yeongjo (r. 1724-1776) was painted in 1900, the 4th year of Gwangmu 광무, when seven royal portraits which had previously been lost in fire at Seonwonjeon Hall 선원전, Hall of Royal Portraits in Gyeongungung 경운궁 Palace (Palace of Joyful Fortune) were reproduced. This portrait was based on the portrait, originally painted in 1744, the 20th year of King Yeongjo's reign, which was enshrined at Yuksanggung 육상궁 Shrine for Concubine Choe 숙빈 최씨, the mother of King Yeongjo. Two court painters, Chae Yongshin 채용신 (1850-1941) and Jo Seokjin 조석진 (1853-1920) were the main painters of this portrait. The half-length figure is wearing a royal winged cap and a red dragon robe, with five-clawed dragon on the chest and shoulder insignias which were embroidered with gold thread. The title was written by Emperor Gojong himself.

서암
Seoam

Originally called Wangam 왕암,
Seoam refers to the rock located behind
Taeryeongjeon. Its name is attributed to a
common saying that Gwanghaegun had
established Gyeonghuigung Palace here.
In 1708 (King Sukjong 34th Year), it was
renamed as Seoam and King Sukjong wrote
thename in Chinese characters in person
and had them engraved on a stone in a grand
fashion.

View from Sujeongjeon. Where exqusite harmony of Korea's past, present, and future exists.

ACKNOLWLEDGMENT

Texts and References

Gwanghwamun	wikipedia.org/wiki/Gwanghwamun
Changdeokgung	wikipedia.org/wiki/Changdeokgung
Changgyeonggung	wikipedia.org/wiki/Changgyeonggung
Dancheong	wikipedia.org/wiki/Dancheong
Gyeonghuigung	wikipedia.org/wiki/Gyeonghuigung, official brochures
Deoksugung	wikipedia.org/wiki/Deoksugung, official brochures
Gyeongbokgung	wikipedia.org/wiki/Gyeongbokgung
Irwolobongdo	wikipedia.org/wiki/Irworobongdo
Jangdokdae	wikipedia.org/wiki/Jangdokdae
Yonggo Drum	wikipedia.org/wiki/Korean_barrel_drum
Eojwa	wikipedia.org/wiki/Phoenix_Throne
Admiral Yi Sun Sin statue	wikipedia.org/wiki/Statue_of_Admiral_Yi_Sun-sin
King Sejong Statue	wikipedia.org/wiki/Statue_of_King_Sejong_(Gwanghwamun)
Japsang	wikipedia.org/wiki/Sungkyunkwan
Shipjangsaeng	wikipedia.org/wiki/Traditional_patterns_of_Korea
Haetae	wikipedia.org/wiki/Xiezhi

Hamnyeongjeon	texts adopted from deoksugung.go.kr
Deokhongjeon	

Taesil
Hwangyeongjeon
Tongmyeongjeon
Jipbokheon
Yeongchunheon
Gwandoekjeong
Gwancheondae
Chundangji
Dongsipjagak
Geonchunmun
Yeongchumun   texts adopted from heritage.co.kr
Geunjeongmun
Heungnyemun
Gibyeolcheong
Seongjeonggak
Saryangjeong
Pyeomusa
Junmyeongdang
Jeonggwanheon

PHOTO CREDIT

heritage.go.kr, licensed under KOGL		Tommy Wong [flickr.com/photos/gracewong (CC BY 2.0)]		영이 [CC BY-SA 3.0 (creativecommons.org/licenses/by-sa/3.0/)]
15	Gibyeolcheong			
17	Geonchunmun	16	Shinmumun	37 Jagyeongjeon
Front, Back, 28	Eojwa	Adam Raoof [flickr.com/photos/adamraoof (CC BY 2.0)]		
160	Hamnyeongjeon_Inside			Ymblanter [CC BY-SA 3.0 (creativecommons.org/licenses/by-sa/3.0/)]
160	Hamnyeongjeon_Ondol			
167	Jeonggwanheon_Pattern_Bat	30	Sajeongjeon	38-39 Geoncheongung
167	Jeonggwanheon_Pattern_Tile	Top6bin [CC BY-SA 4.0 (creativecommons.org/licenses/by-sa/4.0/)]		Stephen Mihalcik, Emeradnabi [CC BY 2.0 (creativecommons.org/licenses/by/2.0/)]
94	Sangryangjeong			
95	Pyeomusa			
106	Munjeongjeon	32	Sujeongjeon	40 Jibokjae
120	Haminjeong_Plate	Joon-Young, Kim [CC BY-SA 3.0 (creativecommons.org/licenses/by-sa/3.0/)]		Rheo1905 [CC BY-SA 4.0 (creativecommons.org/licenses/by-sa/4.0/)]
121	Haminjeong_Roof			
129	Tongmyeongjeon_Yeolcheon			
129	Tongmyeongjeon_Yeonji	22	Geunjeongmun	41 Jaseondang
132	Jipbokheon	Front, 34	Gyotaejeon	
133	Yeongchunheon			
134	Gwandeokjeong	Satomi Abe [flickr.com/photos/abex (CC BY-SA 2.0)]		karendotcom127 [flickr.com/photos/karendotcom127 (CC BY 2.0)]
135	Gwancheondae			
84-85	Seongjeonggak			
112-113	Sungmundang	Front, 35	Amisan	63 Geumcheongyo
116-117	Binyangmun	abex [CC BY-SA 2.0 (creativecommons.org/licenses/by-sa/2.0/)]		70-71 Injeongmun
122-123	Gyeongchunjeon			Back, 83 Daejojeon_Inside
124-125	Hwangyeongjeon			
126-127	Tongmyeongjeon	52	Jagyeongjeon Stonewall	

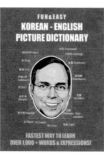

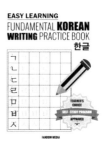
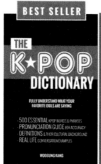

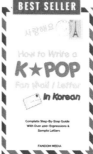

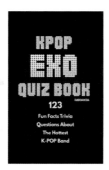

Made in the USA
Monee, IL
29 February 2020